All About Rocks and Minerals

Some rock is as shiny as any glass we manufacture. Some sparkles with flecks of minerals. Some is in six-sided crystals. Some shows the pattern of the tiny seashells from which it is made.

In *All About Rocks and Minerals*, Anne Terry White tells of the vast changes that have produced these different rocks. And she explains how to identify the rocks and minerals that we see around us.

allabout
books

ALL ABOUT
ROCKS AND
MINERALS

BY ANNE TERRY WHITE

ILLUSTRATED BY RENÉ MARTIN

RANDOM HOUSE / NEW YORK

To JUDITH TERRY

Contents

1

The
Commonest Thing
in the World

Rock is the commonest thing in the world.

Who has not picked up a stone and flung it high in the air? Who has not made a pebble skip over the water? We do these things just as naturally as we breathe. We are so used to handling stones and stepping on them and kicking them with our feet, it never occurs to us that rock is the most valuable thing there is.

But isn't that a contradiction—the commonest and the most valuable?

Maybe it sounds that way. But there is no contradiction in it. For nearly everything that makes life possible came out of the rocks.

Much of our air came out of the rocks. Much of our water came out of the rocks and all of our soil did. We often hear someone say of a thing, "It's cheap as dirt." But dirt isn't cheap. We found that out when the wind blew away the top soil of Oklahoma and turned rich farms into wasteland. Everything that lives on land owes its life to the soil, and soil is rock that has decayed. Neither plants nor animals nor we ourselves would be here if it were not for rock.

Do you doubt the value of rock? Look around. You will be startled by the list of common things made of rock or some product of the rock. In five minutes you will count a hundred.

Here is a stone building, a wall, a foundation, stone window trim and steps, a monument, a pier, a bridge, a breakwater. Here are asphalt sidewalks, cement pavements, gravel walks, bricks, curbstones and windowpanes. The mirror over the dresser is a product of the rock. So is the glass from which we drink. So are the dishes on the table. Yes, even the pots, pans, spoons and knives.

For metal, too, comes out of the rocks.

We say with pride, "We live in the Atomic Age."

But for all our progress, we haven't left stone behind. We rely on it even more than cave men did. All they asked of rock was shelter, a few tips for their wooden spears, some knives and scrapers, and pieces of flint to strike fire. But we till the soil. We make thousands of things out of clay and sand. We make thousands of things out of stone. And we use metal. Our cars, planes, rails and machines all go back to the rock.

Rock gave shelter, weapons, tools and fire to the cave man.

All About Our Changing Rocks

The coal we use to smelt our metal is a rock. And even the "gas" and oil that keep our machines running come out of the rocks.

What is this all-important rock? How were the different kinds made? Out of what? Where? When?

A little while ago not even the wisest men on earth could answer any of these questions. People said the rocks had been "created," but that didn't really explain anything.

So the questions kept coming back. The people with inquiring minds racked their brains to solve the mystery of the rocks.

Then about 175 years ago a man came along who said he had the answer. He knew where the rocks had come from. He knew how they had been made.

You may be sure that people opened their ears to listen.

2

Professor
Werner
Has an Idea

The man who "knew" how the rocks had been made was a German. His name was Abraham Gottlob Werner.

Professor Werner really did know a great deal about rocks. He had grown up in an old mining region where everybody's business was getting different materials out of the rocks. Just about the first thing he learned was that these materials were called *minerals* and that there were hundreds of different kinds in the earth. His father had a small collection of them. He told the boy that practically everything in the world except plants and animals was made of minerals. Abraham played with the little pieces of metal and rock in his father's cabinet. Pretty soon he started a collection of his own.

He would go down into the mines to look for rare minerals in cavities of the rocks. And while he was

"Why do rocks lie in layers like books in a pile?" he asked.

looking, he would observe how the different kinds of rock lay in the earth. He saw that they rested one on top of another.

"Why is that?" the boy wondered. "Why do the rocks lie in layers one above another?"

When he went tramping, he kept looking at the rocks and thinking about how they had been made.

"They couldn't have been created suddenly, all at one time," he thought. "I've noticed that in lots of places the rocks lie one on top of another just like books in a pile. I think the bottom layer must have been made first and the other layers put down on top of it *one at a time*."

How could it have happened? What had done it? He thought and thought about it. By the time he had finished school and had become a teacher in Freiburg Academy, he had a theory worked out in his mind.

His subject was minerals and mining. Nobody in the world knew as much about these things as he did; so students flocked to his classroom from the ends of the civilized world. They weren't just young people, either. Many were famous scientists themselves. Many were men who held important positions. They had dropped everything and had taken time out to study German so they could understand what he had to say.

Everybody agreed that Werner was a marvelous

teacher. When he brought out specimens from his collection and talked about them, everybody wanted to have a collection. All of them wanted to go tramping over the world to look for new minerals. But the thing that interested them most was what the professor had to say about how the rocks had been made.

"Open your eyes and look about you," Werner would say. "The rocks themselves will tell you that they weren't made suddenly, all at one time. They aren't thrown together higgledy-piggledy, any which way. There is order in the earth. In many places you will see regular formations—one kind of rock lies in a neat layer on top of another.

"Now, if you found a pile of books lying that way, what would you say? 'Naturally,' you would say, 'the book on the bottom was laid down first and the book on top was laid down last.' So it is with the rocks. The earth's outer zone—which we call its crust—was built gradually, one layer at a time. The lowest layer was made first and the top one last."

And then the professor would go on to tell how he supposed it had been done.

"Once," he would say, "a mighty ocean surrounded the whole earth. It lay miles deep above the con-

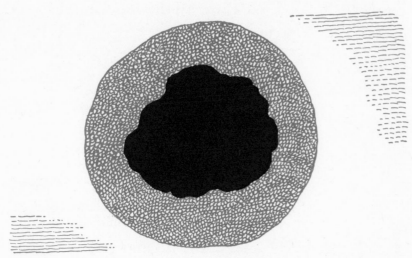

Once a muddy ocean surrounded the core of the earth.

tinents. It covered the tops of the highest mountains. And the water of this ocean was very thick and muddy. For the rocks which now make up the earth's crust were then all a part of this ocean. They were loose particles mixed in the water or dissolved in it.

"As time went on," Professor Werner would say, "this solid matter in the water settled out of it. The granite particles were heaviest. So they settled first. The granite particles covered the entire core of the earth and fitted around it just the way an onion skin fits around an onion. After a time the next heaviest particles settled down. They, too, formed a layer all around the earth. Each kind of particle made a different layer. And that's how all the rocks in the earth's crust were formed."

The students listened spellbound. Everybody who stepped into Werner's classroom accepted his theory. All believed that a vast muddy ocean had once covered the whole earth.

"Yes, certainly," they said. "This theory is sound. It explains the facts. The different rocks do lie in layers. And when you dig down in the earth, under all the other kinds of rock, you do find granite. Things must have happened exactly the way Professor Werner says."

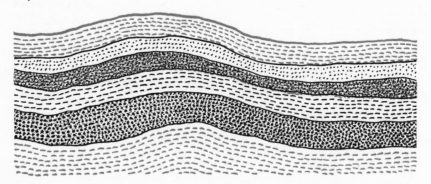

The rocks of the earth lie in vast layers.

3

James
Hutton
Finds the Key

There was something so convincing about Professor Werner that nearly everybody in the world who heard about his ocean came to believe in it. But a few people found it hard to take.

Where had the water of the muddy ocean come from? And where did it go?

James Hutton was one of the unbelievers.

Hutton was a Scotch doctor who had taken to farming, and farming had opened his eyes to the way Nature works. He watched what rain and wind and frost do, and he thought: "Why should we suppose that in the long ago Nature behaved otherwise than she does today? Why should we imagine that she worked with other forces than those she uses now?"

In the spring he saw rain water form into a little rill and run down a bare hillside. The little stream washed away some of the soil and made a gully. Year by year he saw the gully get bigger.

"That's just how the valleys between high mountains must have been made," he thought. "The rivers *dug* them out. Don't people say water will wear away the hardest stone? Water will wear away even the side of a mountain *if we allow time enough.*"

And he remembered a deep, steep gorge he had seen between two mountains. Everybody believed that a terrible accident had ripped the mountain in two.

"We don't need to imagine a terrible accident to account for the gorge," he said. *"The present is the key to the past.* By watching a stream make a gully right now, we can see how the gorge was made long ago. The stream that now runs at the bottom of the gorge must once have run at the very top. The water wore its way down through the mountain and left a gorge behind. Of course, it took a very long time."

In the spring Hutton would watch a river bringing silt and mud and rocks down to the sea. "This waste,"

Hutton realized the water had worn away the earth and stone.

he thought, "is what some of the rocks are made from. Nature hasn't finished the job yet. Out of this material which she is wearing away from the rocks today she will make the rocks of tomorrow."

Hutton became so interested in the question of rocks and time that he finally decided to give up farming altogether. He wanted to devote the rest of his life to science. He wanted to explain once for all the mystery of where the rocks had come from.

The Scotchman was a great walker. He walked all over Scotland looking at the rocks. Quite a number of Werner's pupils were tramping around Europe at the same time looking at the rocks. They were looking for proof that Werner was right. But James Hutton was looking for proof that Werner was wrong.

Most especially he wanted proof that Werner was wrong about granite. Werner had said granite was the first rock that settled out of the muddy ocean. Hutton didn't believe granite had ever had anything to do with water. He believed it had come from deep inside the earth. He knew that hot molten rock comes pouring out of volcanoes today, and he believed gran-

Hutton walked all over Scotland looking at the rocks.

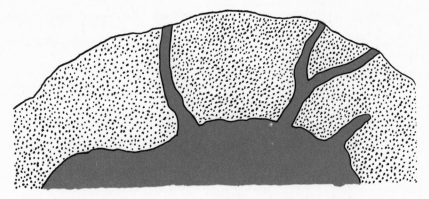

Granite had pushed up to fill the cracks in the rocks.

ite had been made in a similar way—by great heat inside the earth.

How could he prove it?

One day while he was on a rock-exploring trip in Glen Tilt, just north of Edinburgh, Hutton came upon the proof. Before him was a bare hillside with several kinds of rock showing. Down at the bottom of the hill was a mass of red granite. Above the granite were layers of limestone and other rocks. And in the limestone and other rocks were broad cracks filled with red granite.

What was the meaning of those granite-filled cracks?

They could mean just one thing. Granite had flowed up from the mass below and filled the cracks in the rocks above. Now, a solid couldn't have *flowed*. The granite, then, must once have been liquid. It had welled up from inside the earth! It had come up as a *hot* fluid, too, because Hutton could see where it had *baked* the rock close to it!

He was beside himself with joy. He shouted and danced and flung his arms around in front of the wonderful red granite.

His guide looked at him as though he thought the doctor had gone mad. Then he, too, got excited. "Is it gold ye have found?" he demanded.

How could Hutton explain that he had found something much more important than gold! Here was proof that Werner was wrong. Granite had not settled out of a mighty ocean. Like lava, granite had come up boiling hot from the depths of the earth!

The doctor stood in front of the rock and a thousand thoughts ran through his mind. It was a long time before he could tear himself away.

"There is no secret about how the rocks were made," he thought when at last he turned homeward. "Some were made by heat inside the earth. Some were made out of bits worn away from other rocks. We need no ocean full of mud and silt to explain the crust of the earth. *The present is the key to the past.*"

4

War
Against
the Rocks

You might suppose that people would have been very glad to have the mystery of the rocks solved so simply. But not at all.

"Hutton's ideas are simple," people said, "but they are simple nonsense. Why, it would take a million years for a river to cut a gorge through a mountain! So it couldn't possibly have happened that way. Everybody knows that the earth itself is less than 6,000 years old."

But years passed and ideas changed. Proofs came that the earth was vastly older than people thought. One by one Werner's followers went over to Hutton.

All About Our Changing Rocks

It even seemed funny to them that they had ever believed in the muddy ocean.

"Hutton is right," they said. "We mustn't think of the crust of the earth as something finished and done long ago. Nature is still busy making it. She is making rocks right now—making and unmaking them."

And they looked with new eyes at everything around them.

What did they see?

They saw that nothing in the world is two minutes the same. They saw that rock is always and forever changing. Slowly, slowly, all around us it is breaking, crumbling and coming down.

Some changes take place quickly. We can see a gully grow. We can even see a coastline change. If a shore is made of soft materials, we can see it change even from year to year. That's how it is at Cape Cod. The cape and the islands near it are shrinking all the time. Every year the sea eats away from a foot to six feet of the coast. In England the chalk cliffs near Dover are disappearing even faster. In the period of a year the shoreline moves back about fifteen feet.

In other places we can see the coast change only a little bit over a whole lifetime. Year after year we go

Great cliffs along the English Channel are worn by the sea.

back to a shore we know and see no difference. There is the same cliff. There is the same beach. Down at the water's edge is a heap of boulders. It looks as if it had been there always.

And then one day we start talking to an old fisherman perhaps. He points to the heap of boulders.

"I remember when that pile of rock was part of the cliff," he tells us. "It used to stick out like a shelf. Then a big storm came along and brought it down."

We look at the sea that comes rolling in and we try to see how it happened. We watch the waves pick up sand and pebbles and hurl them against the cliff. "How can the rock stand it?" we think.

Then we notice that at the base of the cliff a hollow has formed. The hollow will get bigger and bigger as the waves keep blasting away at it with the pebbles and sand they carry. We can readily see that. After many years the top of the cliff will stick out like a shelf, and there will be nothing underneath to hold it up. Then a storm will come. Furious waves will pound against the cliff. The shelf will come crashing down. It will break into a thousand pieces and lie in a heap at the bottom. It will be just like that other heap of rocks over which the sea is washing now.

We pick up some of the pebbles on the shore. We let the warm, dry sand run through our fingers. It is hard to believe that once the pebbles and sand were all part of the cliffs. But we can see the waves working to make the fallen rocks always smaller. We can see how the pebbles become rounded and smooth. Every wave picks up and rolls the little stones over and over and grinds them against one another. Sooner or later the sharp corners must wear off. With a start we realize that this sand which runs so pleasantly through our fingers is a mass of those sharp little corners that have broken off!

Shorelines change. We can see many of them doing

Waves blast at the cliffs with the rocks and sand they carry.

21

it. But there are other changes in the rocks which we cannot see—even in a lifetime, even in many lifetimes. The mountains always look the same to us. We can see no change in them even in a thousand years. And yet, like the shore, they are not the same for even two minutes. Between the time you started reading this page and the time you finish it, every mountain in the world will have changed a tiny bit.

"But if you can't see the changes, how do you know there are any?" you might ask.

There are many proofs that the mountains change. The simplest of all is a proof you can see for yourself the next time you are near a mountain.

Here is a mountain now. It looks just as it did in Columbus' day. But at the foot lies a heap of broken rock and sand. Up on the slope there is another heap. There is your evidence that the mountain is changing. This is the proof that slowly, slowly, it is wearing away.

The heaps came from the mountain, of course. We can see that they are made up of bits of the mountain that have *weathered* off. That ocean of air above us, which we call the atmosphere and think so beautiful with its blue color and white clouds, is a great enemy

Even sun, rain and air cause mountains to wear away.

of rock. It has been eating away at the mountain. The oxygen in the air joined up with certain elements in the rock and formed new substances which made the rock much weaker. Carbon dioxide joined with other elements and weakened the rock some more. Then rain came. The water got into the pores of the rock. It dissolved some of the materials in the rock and carried them away. Slowly the rock rotted.

In the daytime the sun beat down. The rocks expanded from the heat, then at night they contracted from the cold. Over and over again this happened, for years and years. Finally the rocks cracked. Dew formed on the outside; rain water seeped into the cracks. It is cold on a mountain even in summer. At night the water froze in the pores and crevices of the rock. As the water turned into ice, it expanded and pressed hard against the walls. Large chunks and small chunks broke off. They rolled down to the bottom of the slope. There the pieces lie in a cone-shaped heap which scientists call a *talus*.

"How long," you ask, "did it take for air and rain and sun and frost and wind to wear away this much of the mountain?"

A long time. Thousands of years certainly. For almost nothing in the world changes as slowly as a mountain. A mountain may come down as much as four inches in a thousand years—and that's only about a quarter of an inch in a lifetime.

5

Where
Did the Boulders
Come From?

Perhaps you have been to New England. If you have, you couldn't help noticing what a stony part of the world it is. Every old farm is fenced in with stone walls. The pastures are full of boulders, some of them as big as a house. But they are not part of the bedrock. The boulders have been brought from many miles away.

Once those transported rocks were a great mystery to everybody. "How on earth did they get here?" people wondered. "Something must have brought them. But what?"

For a long time people thought the boulders must

have been swept to New England by Noah's flood. It wasn't sensible to think that, but there was nothing else they could blame the boulders on. Then about a hundred years ago a Swiss college professor named Louis Agassiz got on the right track.

There were just such boulders in the valleys of his own country. And there were just such boulders frozen into the glaciers in the Swiss Alps. "Maybe," he thought, "it is warmer in the valleys now than it used to be. Maybe at one time the glaciers extended 'way down. Perhaps they melted and left behind the boulders they were carrying."

Agassiz decided he'd watch and see how a glacier behaved. So he had a hut built on top of a glacier, invited some friends to join him, and moved in. The friends came—they didn't want to miss an exciting adventure like that even though things promised to be crowded and uncomfortable.

They came, and for months everybody watched the glacier. They bored holes in the ice and let thermometers down to see how cold the glacier was at this depth and that. With surveying instruments they marked the position of eighteen big boulders caught in the ice. Agassiz meant to watch the boulders year

Agassiz observed the great boulders caught in the glacier.

after year and see how fast the glacier moved.

The professor learned a lot about glaciers. Long before the adventure was over he came to the conclusion that Hutton was right when he said, "The present is the key to the past."

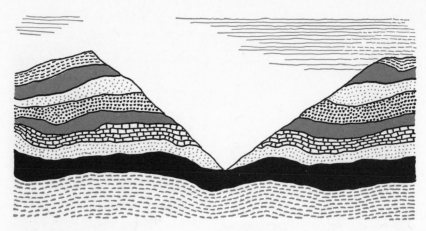

Before the glacier went through, the valley was V-shaped.

Agassiz saw that what glaciers are doing today they did thousands of years ago—only long ago they did it on a much bigger scale. He understood that a great icecap—like the one that lies over Greenland today—had once lain over most of northern Europe, all of Canada, and the northern part of the United States.

The professor came to America to look at the New England boulders, too. He said the glacier had gathered them up and carried them along as it moved south.

How did the glacier do it?

A glacier works just like a plow. But instead of one blade, it has a thousand. For every rock frozen into its bottom acts like a plowshare. As the glacier moves

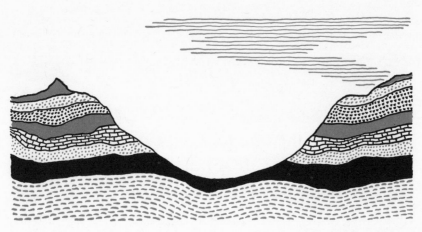

The glacier smoothed the valley until it is shaped like a U.

along, the rocks frozen into it keep prying up other pieces of rock.

But that isn't the whole story. The ice itself bites off and carries away tons upon tons of rock.

That happens especially when a glacier flows into a valley. For in a valley the ice is shut in between mountain walls. Water seeps into the cracks of the walls, freezes and expands. Huge chunks of rock break off. They fall down on top of the ice, and the glacier carries them along as if it were a sled.

Anybody can recognize a valley through which a glacier has passed. The glacier has plucked so much rock from the mountain walls and plowed up so much rock from the valley floor that the sides and bottom become rounded like a trough. Before the glacier went through the Yosemite Valley, it was shaped like a V. Now it is shaped like a U.

Glaciers look so harmless. Glaciers creep so slowly. But wherever they go, they leave their mark on the rocks. The Yosemite is not the only valley they have changed from a V to a U. They have dug out hundreds of valleys. They have smoothed down countless mountains. They have brought down and scattered boulders over hundreds of thousands of square miles. They have gouged out many of the lakes in the world today.

Glaciers are the constant enemy of rock.

Many boulders in New England were carried down by glacier.

6

Down, Down, Down.

Down, down, down. Everywhere around us rock is breaking, crumbling, and coming down.

We go for a ride and near a height we see a sign: "Watch out for fallen rocks." The mountains are coming down.

We pick up a newspaper and read, "Landslide wipes out village." The hills are coming down.

We see a gang of men setting out vines upon a roadside slope. They are planting a cover of growing things to hold the soil in place. Without this, the whole thing would come tumbling down.

Every gorge, every valley shows us that rock is

crumbling and coming down. Every river carrying waste to the sea shows us the same.

Out in our Southwest lies a great natural wonder— the Grand Canyon of the Colorado River. Every year thousands of tourists come from all over the world to see it. But though they "oh" and "ah" over the sight, not many really understand what it is they are looking at. The Grand Canyon of the Colorado is the world's most gigantic example of rocks destroyed by water and wind and air.

You stand on the rim of the Grand Canyon and look out. Before you is a giant chasm that stretches as far as you can see. It is more than eight miles wide. It is three hundred miles long. And it is a mile deep. Down at the bottom flows the Colorado River which looks quite unimportant.

You look out and it seems to you that what you are seeing is not a chasm but two ranges of mountains. The top of each mountain is flat, and each is made of layer upon layer of rock. You can see the layers distinctly, for they are of different colors—some red, some green, some gray, some white. The whole scene looks as if it were cut out of gaily colored cardboard.

What does it all mean? What is the explanation of

this wonder?

That unimportant looking river a mile below you is responsible for what has happened here. Once there was no chasm. The river flowed at the level where you stand. The Colorado is a very muddy river. It has used its silt and mud and stones as tools to saw and drill and grind its way down through a mile of rock. The streams that flow into the Colorado have cut the side

From the rim of the Grand Canyon you can see the Colorado River grinding its way through layer upon layer of rock.

canyons. With the help of air and rain and sun and frost and wind, the Colorado River and its tributaries have carved mountains out of the Colorado Plateau. It took a million years for them to do it.

How much rock did they destroy in that time?

You can get some notion of it from how much rock waste the Colorado carries away right now. Every hour it takes to the sea 11,000 tons of mud and stones! It has been doing that twenty-four hours a day, seven days a week for a million years!

But this is not the end yet. This is only a halfway point, for the Colorado and its tributaries are still sawing and drilling and grinding. Bit by bit the mountains will shrink still more. Bit by bit they will be carried out to sea. It is the fate of all mountains to disappear. It is the fate of these mountains.

7

The
Land
Fights Back

"But if rock has been breaking, crumbling, and coming down for millions of years," you might ask, "how is it that there are still mountains that are miles high?"

The answer is simple. Our mountains, though they seem so old to us, are really still quite new. Nature hasn't had time yet to bring them down to sea level the way she has brought down other, much older, mountains that were here earlier. Give Nature time and she will wear the Rockies down like all the rest!

Right now North America stands high above the sea. But it hasn't always been like that. Time after time our continent has been worn down so low that shallow seas washed over it. Sometimes almost all of North America has been under the sea—it looked more like a lot of islands than a continent. But always the land has come up again.

For rock is made as well as unmade. Rock is lifted up as well as brought down. Though mountains wear away, new ones always build up again.

To be sure, they take their time about it. Mountains for the most part go up very, very slowly. There is only one kind that springs up fast. That's a volcano.

In 1943 we had a chance to find out just how fast a volcano can come up. For that year a brand new one was born in a Mexican corn field. A farmer by the name of Dionisio Polido was plowing the field at the time and saw the volcano from the moment it started.

Dionisio said that he saw a little smoke coming out of a low place in the field. He thought his last cigarette stub had set some cornstalks on fire and went over to see. The smoke was pouring from a crack in the ground. As he stood there looking, the ground began to shake and with a roar cracked wide open. A wild wind caught up his hat and carried it high into the air.

In 1943 a new volcano broke out in a Mexican corn field.

He was terribly frightened, he said, and ran away. But he did turn to look back. Rocks were shooting out of the earth like a fountain. It was just as though someone inside the earth were hurling rocks into the sky.

By the time Dionisio had brought the priest and some other brave men to see the wonder, so much smoking rock had fallen back down around the opening that the pile was as high as a tree. People stood at the edge of the corn field and watched the volcano all night long. By morning the pile was 200 feet high!

Parícutin, as the Mexicans named the volcano, kept growing and growing. A whole week passed before anything else happened. And then melted rock began to flow out. Before Parícutin stopped working, it leaked millions of tons of liquid rock. And the mountain itself kept on growing till it was 1,600 feet high.

We don't know if all volcanic mountains started the same way as Parícutin. But we know that all of them were built out of rock that came pouring from their own throats. We call the big solid pieces that shoot out *bombs*. We call the small ones *cinders*. And we call the liquid rock *lava*. But we also have a name for *all* rocks that come from inside the earth. We call all of them *igneous rocks*.

Igneous means *fire-made*. The word is a hang-over from long ago when people thought there was fire inside the earth. They thought it was hollow and that wild winds rushing around in the underground caverns struck fire from the rocks. Now we know there isn't any fire inside the earth, though it is certainly hot enough there to melt rock. But we keep on calling all rock that comes up from the earth's interior *igneous*.

It took nine years for Parícutin to build a cone

A volcano is built of rock that came out of its own throat.

It takes thousands of years for a high volcano to build itself up.

1,600 feet high. How long did it take to build a really
high volcano like Mount Vesuvius in Italy?

Probably it took many thousands of years. For we
know that a big cone doesn't shoot up all at one time.
Sometimes there are long periods of quiet between
lava flows. Sometimes a volcano sleeps for a thousand
years and then suddenly starts spouting lava again.

But dome-shaped volcanoes go up even more
slowly than the big cones. For the lava that makes
them is more liquid and flows right away from the
opening. It takes many, many flows for even a little

dome to be built up. Yet think of it! There are dome volcanoes higher than any of the cones. The Hawaiian Islands are huge dome volcanoes. Those islands are mountains which have been built up by lava flows from the floor of the deep ocean.

Many, many islands of the Pacific have been built up by lava flows. Some in the Atlantic have, too. Iceland, for example, is a volcanic island; and only 200 years ago it had a great lava flow. Then twenty-two

Many islands in the Pacific were built by lava flows.

cracks, or fissures, opened up in the ground. Lava flowed and flowed out of them. It seemed as if the lava would never stop.

But that Iceland flow was nothing compared to some of the fissure flows that took place long ago. There was a time when in our own country lava came up through cracks in the earth and spread like a sea over western Washington and Oregon and Idaho. That sea of rock covered an area bigger than all New England. In spots the lava was a mile deep. In Wyoming flow after flow of lava built up the plateau where Yellowstone Park stands today. And on other continents it was the same. In Uruguay and Brazil and India, lava built up plateaus even more vast.

8

Up,
Up,
Up.

Volcanoes are certainly spectacular. And compared with other natural forces they are fast. But if we had to depend on lava to keep the land high, the sea would always win.

Luckily something else is busy making mountains and plateaus. Many of them are not *built* up but simply *pushed* up. And this happens because rock is not really as rigid as it looks.

Of course, if you pick up a rock and try to bend it, you won't succeed. But rock will bend, the way steel will bend, if there is sufficient force pressing slowly.

Now, inside the earth that kind of pressure is being

applied somewhere all the time. When the pressure is great enough, the layers of rock in the earth bend. But if the pressure is too great, the rock can't take it and snaps. It snaps and moves into a new position to relieve the strain.

When that happens down in the earth, we up on the surface feel the ground shake. Sometimes nothing else happens up where we are. But sometimes the rock breaks all the way to the top. We can *see* the break then.

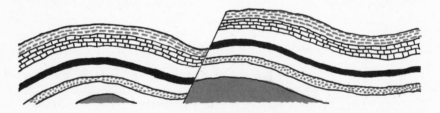

Sometimes the rock breaks so there is a gap between the pieces. Sometimes it breaks so that the pieces slide in different directions along a crack. We call such places where rock has broken and moved apart *faults*. A fault may measure only a few inches or a few feet at first. But as more and more faulting occurs in the same place, the break may come to be thousands of feet apart or even several miles.

Sometimes one end of the broken rock keeps moving up and up till we have a great mountain, steep on one side and gently sloping on the other like this.

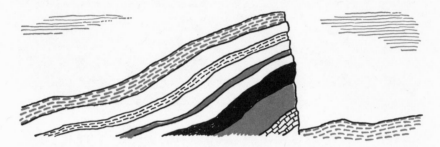

Sometimes faulting occurs in two places, and a block of rock rises straight up like this

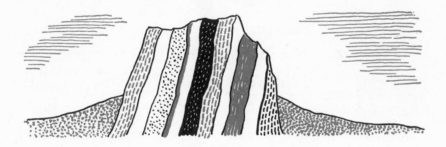

or may be tilted like this

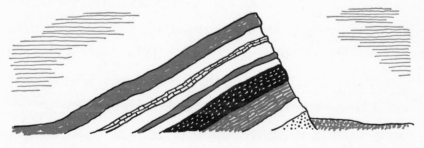

Sometimes a whole great area is faulted in this way

and block mountains of different heights stick up all over it like this.

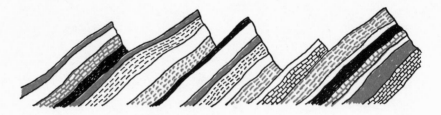

We have that kind of mountains in the Great Basin of Nevada. Each of them sticks up out of the earth the way a brick may tilt up out of its place in an old brick walk. Each mountain is a huge separate block of rock that has been lifted up.

The Sierra Nevada Mountains of California are like that, too. That whole range of mountains is just one enormous tilted block. The block is 400 miles long and 60 miles wide. On the side facing the Pacific the great block mountain slopes gently. On its eastern side it is very steep and in places goes up more than two miles above the desert.

You may be sure the Sierras didn't get that high suddenly. The tilting of that great block of rock was not one movement but many. For though a cliff has been known to move up fifty feet at one time, it doesn't happen that way very often.

9

A
Sea Floor
Comes Up

Once, when people were just beginning to understand the rocks, a naturalist found some sea shells on top of the Andes Mountains. He was astonished. How did sea shells get into rocks miles high in the air? Sea shells could mean just one thing—the sea. "But it were madness to think the sea was ever here!" he exclaimed. He couldn't believe it.

Today we know it isn't madness to think that a sea once rolled where the Andes stand. We know that a sea a thousand miles wide once flowed where the Rockies stand. A sea flowed where the Appalachians stand. The Himalayas, the Alps, the Andes have all come up out of the sea.

Scientists don't agree as to *why* Nature should do this strange thing—why she should choose to lift up a sea floor and make it over into mountains. But all are of one mind about *how* it happens. It starts, they tell us, with the gathering of a vast amount of sediment on the floor of a sea.

Of course, sediment collects on every sea floor. For streams and rivers, bringing sediment and pebbles, empty into the seas. This is the end of their journey. It is here that the waves spread out the rock bits they have knocked and battered off the coast as well as those that streams have carried to the sea. But there are some seas that have received an *exceptional*

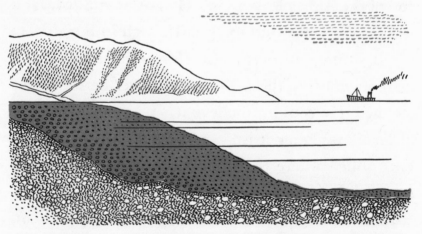

Streams and rivers bring pebbles and sediment into the seas.

Our greatest mountains all rose from the floor of the sea.

amount of sediment. The seas that flowed where the great mountain ranges of the world now stand were seas like that.

How does it happen? How does a sea floor come up?

Let us squeeze millions of years into a couple of pages and see. . . .

We watch the waves come and go. Endlessly they pick up and drop the waste. But all the time they are playing with the pebbles and sand and mud, the waves sort them out. The coarse material is the heaviest. So as the waves go out, they drop the pebbles first, right near the shore. The sand they take a little farther out. The mud is the lightest—the waves carry it farthest out to sea.

Sometimes, however, a storm comes. Then there is a strong undertow. It carries the coarse material farther out into deeper water and lays pebbles and sand down on top of the fine materials laid there when the sea was calm. Fine layer, coarse layer, fine layer, coarse layer—the pile of rock waste gets thicker and thicker.

The sediments are heavy. They weigh down on the sea floor. The time comes when so much rock waste is piled up that the load is too heavy. Then slowly the

Endlessly the waves pick up and drop pebbles, sand and mud.

floor of the sea begins to sink. And all the time it is
sinking, more sediments pile up—the rivers keep
dropping their loads, the waves keep adding what they
themselves have battered from the shore. The waves
tear down, play and sort, play and sort.

The sediments get thicker and thicker on the floor
of the sea. They get to be miles thick. All the lower
layers have turned to rock now. They are no longer
loose sand and mud and pebbles and boulders. The
weight of the sediments on top has pressed them down
and packed them tight. Water has deposited mineral
matter in the open spaces between the particles of
sediment. The mineral matter is pressed so tight
that it cements everything together. *The sediments
have become sedimentary rock.*

All About Our Changing Rocks

And now a pushing begins. It is not like the pushing that made the block mountains. The pushing isn't up. There will be upward pushing later on, much later on. The first pushing comes from the side.

The rock bends and starts to fold like this:

The folds reach into the air, they go down into the earth. The layers of rock that once were so flat look like a washboard now.

What has happened to the sea meantime? It has vanished, its waters have drained off into the deep ocean basin. The sea floor is a low range of mountains now. It stands waiting to be pushed up—waiting to play its part in the struggle against rain and wind, air, ice, waves, and running water.

10

About Minerals

How shall we know the rocks?

We recognize a tree by its fruit, by its leaves, by its bark. We know a bird by its size, shape, color, song. By what shall we recognize the rocks? They have no special shape or size. Lots of different rocks are the same color and most rocks can be many different colors. From season to season rocks stay the same— they don't shed leaves, or bear seeds, build nests, lay eggs. Rocks don't *do* anything—they have no *habits*. So how can we tell what they are?

In part we have to recognize them by the size, shape, and arrangement of their grains. Sometimes we can identify a rock by its hardness. Sometimes we can tell what a rock is just by the way it breaks.

But often we have to identify rocks by the minerals of which they are made.

We identify a rock by the size and shape of its grains.

If you take a piece of granite in your hands and look at it closely, you will see at once what we mean by minerals. Granite is a speckled rock. You will notice that it is made up of grains roughly of the same size, but some of them are light and some are dark. Some of the light specks will look to you like glass, others will have smooth surfaces. With your fingernail you will be able to peel off a few dark paper-thin flakes. Other dark specks won't come off.

Clearly granite is a mixture of several *different* things. Like a fruit cake that contains raisins, currants, citron and nuts, granite is a mixture of several ingredients that are easily recognized. Each of these ingredients is a mineral.

Perhaps the particular piece of granite in your hands will be a mixture of four minerals—quartz, feldspar, mica and hornblende. The light, glassy ones will be quartz; the light ones with smooth surfaces will be feldspar. The dark specks which you can peel off with your fingernail will be black mica. The other dark specks will be hornblende.

But if, now, instead of a piece of granite you pick up a piece of some other kind of rock, you will find that it is a different combination of minerals. It may have, three, four, or a dozen minerals in it. Or, again, you might find that your specimen is made of just one mineral. Marble would be made of just one mineral— calcite. Rock salt would be made of just one mineral— halite.

"Do we, then, have to know all the minerals in order to know the rocks?" you ask.

Definitely not. And that's lucky because there are between thirteen and fourteen hundred different minerals in the earth's crust. We don't need to know the rare ones—they don't make up the common rocks. To know the common rocks we need to get acquainted only with the common rock-forming minerals—that is, with the minerals that make up such ordinary rocks as granite and limestone and schist.

There aren't very many such minerals. To start with, a dozen will be enough. At the back of this book you will find them listed and described. So when you come across the name of a new mineral, you can, if you like, look it up. And when you start your own rock collection, you can refer to the list and check your mineral against the description.

Very often in those descriptions you will meet the word *crystal*. For nearly all minerals form crystals. That is, the atoms of which a mineral is made arrange themselves according to a regular plan.

In one way all the plans are alike—all crystals have flat faces and very sharp angles. Indeed, a crystal that gets room to grow and time to grow in has faces so smooth and angles so well formed that it looks like something cut by a jeweler's tools. But every mineral has its own particular plan. So knowing the plan which a mineral uses helps you to recognize it. Quartz, for example, always makes crystals with six sides and a pointed cap. Mica has six-sided crystals, too, but they are flat.

Color helps some and the general appearance of the mineral helps, and its cleavage—the way it splits, that is. But two things you will find more helpful than any of these.

Quartz

Mica

Diamond

Talc

Calcite

Gypsum

Fluorite

Orthoclase

Topaz

Apatite

Corundum

All crystals have flat faces and very sharp angles.

All About Our Changing Rocks

One is hardness. By this we don't mean how hard it is to break the mineral. A diamond is the hardest mineral there is and yet a light blow from a hammer may shatter it. By the hardness of a mineral we mean how hard it is to scratch. A scale of hardness has been worked out in ten degrees. The easiest to scratch is No. 1 (Talc) and the hardest is No. 10 (Diamond). Each mineral in the scale will scratch the one before it, but can't be scratched by it.

Hardness 1. Talc   6. Orthoclase
Scale   2. Gypsum   7. Quartz
              3. Calcite   8. Topaz
              4. Fluorite   9. Corundum
              5. Apatite   10. Diamond

Now, you don't need to own a set of these ten minerals in order to test for hardness. You can have a homemade scale. It will consist of your fingernail, a copper penny, a knife, a piece of glass, and a bit of quartz. These five will do nearly as well as the minerals to test the first eight degrees of hardness. And hardly anything is harder than hardness 8. The homemade scale will go like this:

Degree of Hardness Test

1. You can easily scratch the mineral with your fingernail.

2. You can just barely scratch it with your fingernail.

3. You can just barely scratch it with a copper penny.

4. You can easily scratch it with a knife, but not with a penny. The mineral will not scratch glass.

5. You can just barely scratch the mineral with a knife. It will just barely scratch glass.

6. You can't scratch the mineral with a knife at all, but it will scratch glass easily.

7. The mineral will scratch both your knife and glass.

8. The mineral can scratch quartz.

All About Our Changing Rocks

So much for hardness. Now for the other very helpful thing. It is what we call *streak*. By this we mean the color that a mineral makes when you rub it against a piece of unglazed porcelain—the back of an ordinary bathroom tile, for instance. For, strangely, the streak a mineral makes is often quite different from the color of the mineral itself. A mineral may be black, yet its streak may be yellow. Or it may be green, yet make a white streak. Thus, streak is much more dependable than color because impurities in a mineral may change its color.

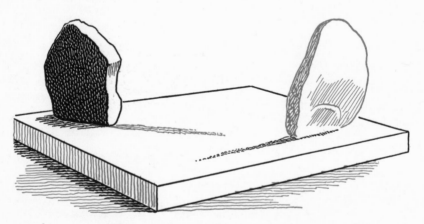

The streak of a mineral tells us more than its color.

11

King
of the
Rocks

Everybody has seen granite. There is so much of it in the world, and it is used for so many things! No matter how far a town may be from a granite region, it is bound to have at least one monument of granite. The chances are you'll find it standing proudly in the square where passing tourists stop to read the inscription: "So and so did such and such."

But what if the granite could speak of itself? What story would it tell?

Every piece of granite would tell of underground adventures. For granite, though we often see it on the surface, is not a native of the top. Like all the igneous rocks, granite is cooked in the hot, dark kitchens of the earth. Like all the igneous rocks it comes up from below as a molten, steaming mass which we call *magma*. But granite magma doesn't pour out on top of the earth like lava. It goes part way up and stops. It stops and lies there, betwixt and between, not up and not down, cooling and forming crystals, and making itself into firm, hard rock. Only after sun and wind and air and water have worn away the rocks above it, does granite see the light of day.

What makes the molten rock come up? How scientists would like to know what starts magma on its journey! All they know is that it does come up. They think it eats its way up. Hot and filled with gases as it is, magma can easily do that.

Sometimes magma finds room for itself between layers of sedimentary rock and spreads out there like

Often the magma spreads between layers of sedimentary rock.

The Mount Rushmore Memorial is carved in solid granite.

a sheet. Sometimes it worms itself into up-and-down cracks in the rocks above and fills them, making wide *dikes* and narrow *veins*. Sometimes a mass of magma eats its way up almost to the very top and spreads out there. Then like the filling of a pie that pushes up the top crust, the magma arches up the layer of rock above. With its neck going straight down and its dome-shaped body, the lake of magma looks like a huge mushroom.

Nearly all the magma that doesn't get to the very top becomes granite. So you can see how much granite there must be in the world. Indeed, the continents are mostly granite. Even the folded mountains which we watched being made out of sedimentary rock are largely granite inside. For magma pushes its way into their folds and turns into a solid there.

Some granite rocks are so huge and go down into the earth so deep that their floors have never been found. Such rocks are called granite *batholiths, deep rocks*. There are granite batholiths that stretch for miles and miles. One group of batholiths—the biggest of all—covers two million square miles!

That is one of the oldest rocks we know. It stretches over part of Canada and is called the Canadian Shield because it is shaped something like a shield. Geologists used to think that perhaps the Canadian Shield was part of the very first crust that ever was formed. But we know now that the scientists were wrong. All the rocks of that *first* crust are gone. They have all been made over into sedimentary rock. The Canadian Shield is just a group of huge batholiths of long, long ago.

"But," you may ask, "if all granite is made the same way, why isn't it all the same color?"

Because magmas aren't all alike. It is the kind of feldspar in the magma that determines the color of the granite, so granite can be many colors. Though most often you will see it gray or pink, it may also be yellow or green. And you will remember that

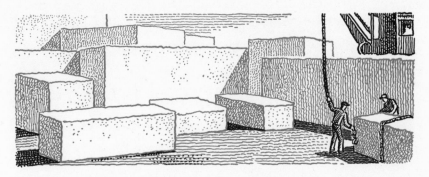

Granite may be gray, pink, yellow, green or red.

Hutton's famous granite was red.

"Yes, but I've seen some granite with grains the size of peas," you may say. "And all granite isn't that coarse. What makes some coarse and some not?"

All granite is grainy—that's why it is called *granite*. But some, to be sure, has bigger grains than others. And that is largely a question of how long a time the crystals had to grow.

For crystals are curious things—they need *time* to grow. As long as the magma is very hot, they can't form at all. But when it starts to cool, the crystals start forming. They grow by adding one little bit to another. The longer magma takes to cool, the more time the crystals have to grow, and the bigger they get. As a rule, the magma deep down in the earth cools more slowly and forms larger crystals. Granite crystals can be as small as a grain of sand. They can be the size of a pea. And they can be much, much bigger.

There is one kind of granite that has crystals many feet long and weighing tons. This rock is called *pegmatite,* or *giant granite.* There is pegmatite in Maine that has feldspar crystals twenty feet long. One giant feldspar crystal that was mined out of a North Carolina pegmatite filled two freight cars. A single mica crystal weighed ninety tons.

Naturally, because its crystals are so big, pegmatite is very valuable. Its feldspar is mined for glazing china. Its mica is used for electrical insulation. Pegmatite also has important minerals besides the usual ones in granite. There is topaz and beryl. And radium is taken out of another ingredient.

Granite is a wonderfully strong rock. Just look at a piece through a magnifying glass and you will understand why.

You will see that some of the minerals are perfect crystals, with smooth sides and sharp angles, while others are irregular. These irregular ones don't even have flat faces and sharp angles. That's because the minerals didn't all form at the same time.

Some of the crystals in granite are perfect, others are not.

As the magma cooled, the first mineral to start making crystals was hornblende. It had plenty of room to form in; so it formed perfect crystals. The black mica crystallized next. It didn't make such perfect crystals because there were neighbors that got in the way. The feldspar separated out next and formed still less perfect crystals. The quartz filled in the spaces between the other minerals. The result is that everything in granite is tightly locked together—which is what makes it so strong.

Because it is strong, granite is one of the most useful rocks in the world. It makes sturdy foundations. It makes strong piers. It makes good sea walls to keep back pounding waves. Granite can also be cut into almost any shape and will take a high polish. So it is used a great deal for monuments and buildings.

Granite is the very King of Rocks.

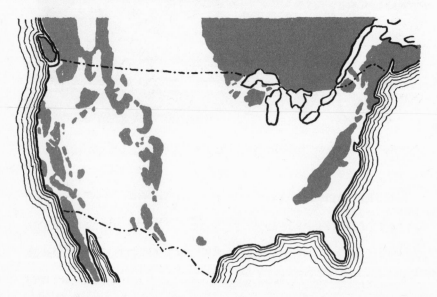

Granite is found in the areas which are shown in color.

12

Two
Lava
Rocks

Just take a look at the map on page 68. You will see that there is lots of granite in the East and in the West. But because granite doesn't come into the open till its cover of sedimentary rocks has worn off, large parts of our country have no granite of their own to show. In the Mississippi Valley there is almost none. Granite is still a "hidden" rock there. It is hidden very far down under all the other rocks.

As a matter of fact, the central part of our country isn't a good place to look for *any* of the igneous rocks. For even those that did get to the top aren't to be found there. The lava rocks are nearly all out West.

In Fingal's Cave in Scotland you will see giant columns of basalt.

When basalt cools, it may shrink and crack into six-sided columns.

It is in the West that the fissure flows were greatest. And it is in the West that our volcanoes poured out their lavas.

It may surprise you, perhaps, to hear that there are volcanoes in America, but we have quite a few of them. Counting big ones and little ones, there are hundreds. Most of them, to be sure, are dead, and we don't expect they'll ever give us any trouble. Some are so old and have been worn down so much that there is nothing left of them except the neck.

However, Mount Lassen in California blew up not so long ago—in 1915. And Mount Hood in Oregon and Mount Rainier in Washington may still be active. They don't look as if they'll send up any fireworks; yet we can't definitely say they are dead, for they are still warm in spots. Mount Vesuvius looked a lot deader before it suddenly came alive—and it had been sleeping for a thousand years.

The rocks that touched any cooling surface—the wall of a dike, for example, or the air above ground—are all much finer-grained than granite. You will see that best when you break a piece of lava rock open. It won't be grainy like granite but will have a velvety look. Generally you will find the lava rocks are so fine-grained that you won't be able to pick out the individual grains without a magnifying glass. And sometimes not even then.

Yet very often you will see in among the tiny crystals some large ones standing out like raisins in a cake. Then you will know your rock is a *porphyry*. If you see big crystals, you know the rock cooled slowly. If you see little, poorly formed crystals, you know it cooled rapidly. You will find that many of the igneous rocks are like that—many igneous rocks are porphyries. Even granite can be a porphyry. So you will have to identify your rock in other ways before you can decide what *kind* of porphyry it is.

Of all the lava rocks, *basalt* is perhaps the darkest common rock. Often it is dark gray or dark green, brown, or even black. This is the lava rock you are most likely to find because it is the commonest lava rock there is. In the Northwest much of it is crushed and used to make hard surfaces for the roads.

The biggest stretch of basalt in America is in Washington, Oregon and Idaho. For the entire Columbia River Plateau was built up by basalt flows. But smaller patches appear in other places. At Paterson, New Jersey, there are famous basalt quarries. There are basalt quarries in the Connecticut Valley, too. The Palisades of the Hudson River Valley were built up by a basalt flow. And in other parts of the world there are stretches of basalt even greater than the Columbia Plateau. In India basalt lies almost two miles deep in spots.

Yet great as are the basalt areas that we can see, those we can't see are greater still. For the ocean basins are all basalt.

A hundred and fifty years ago basalt was a great mystery to geologists. They couldn't understand why it often was in the form of columns with six sides. They would go to look at the Giant's Causeway in Ireland or Fingal's Cave in Scotland and wonder: "Are these great columns giant crystals?"

We have the answer now. Often when basalt cools, it shrinks and cracks up and down into columns which, as a rule, have six sides. This happens sometimes to rock underground as well. Sometimes when molten rock spreads in sheets very close to the top, it, too, cracks up into columns. Then when the sedimentary rocks above have been worn away, a wall of rock columns comes into view.

Andesite is another of the common lava rocks which

you may find. It is a little lighter than basalt and may be many different colors—even pink, red and purplish.

Andesite got its name from the Andes Mountains because that is where geologists first studied and described it. But there is lots of andesite in our own country. Mount Rainier is mostly andesite. Mount Shasta has erupted andesite. So has Mount Taylor, an old volcano in New Mexico. But the greatest andesite regions are Colorado and Wyoming. The whole plateau on which Yellowstone Park stands today was built up by flows of andesite.

If you go to the Yellowstone, you will see the record of those flows in the Amethyst Cliffs. In the side of the cliffs are the remains of eighteen forests standing

Tree stumps, turned to stone, are in the Petrified Forest.

one on top of another! They are fossil forests. Only the stumps of the trees are left. They have turned to stone—petrified, as we say.

Boiling hot rock pouring out of fissures was the enemy that murdered those forests. Millions of years ago it spread over this whole region and killed every living thing. Time passed—tens, hundreds of years passed. Water filled with mineral matter seeped through the rock. Molecule by molecule the mineral matter took the place of the particles of wood. Slowly the tree trunks turned to stone, slowly the lava weathered into soil. And a new forest sprang up on top. Then again the molten rock spread over everything. Eighteen times it did this. Eighteen times, boiling hot lava wiped out everything in sight.

The stone stumps remain to tell the story. The Amethyst Cliffs are a single clear page in the *Record of Living Things* the rocks have kept.

13

Glass
Rocks

Perhaps you once read the fairy tale about the princess who could be won only by the man who was able to ride up a glass hill. When you read it, you probably decided there couldn't be such a thing as a glass hill. But there really is one. There is a glass hill in Yellowstone Park. It was made by lava that cooled very, very quickly. The lava cooled so fast that no crystals had a chance to form. The lava became natural glass.

Such glass made by Nature in her outdoor workshop is called *obsidian*. It is a very handsome igneous rock, found in many parts of the world. Generally it is black, but there is gray, brown, and red obsidian also.

This is one rock you will have no difficulty in recognizing. It is as shiny as any glass we manufacture. You can see through a chip of it as you can through any man-made glass. And at the place where it breaks, the rock is curved somewhat like a giant snail shell. Its edges may be sharp enough to cut your finger.

Obsidian is a rock with a very long history. Stone Age Man chipped it into tools and weapons. The Indians of our West made it into knives and arrowheads. Before that the Mound Builders used it.

Mound Builders walked thousands of miles to get obsidian.

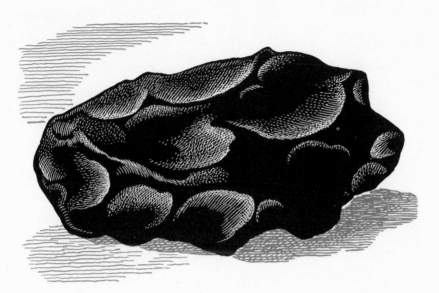

Obsidian is as shiny as any glass we manufacture.

Those ancient, forgotten Indians who built the huge, mysterious burial mounds between the Mississippi and the Alleghenies prized obsidian more than any other stone. They used it only for religious purposes. They would go all the way to the Yellowstone for it—a thousand miles there and a thousand miles back! They would go on foot and bring home a chunk of obsidian on their backs. Then they would cut the stone up into ceremonial knives which were used only when the priests made sacrifices to their gods.

Not all volcanic glass is beautiful like obsidian.

There is another kind that isn't handsome at all and doesn't even look like glass. It is called *pumice*.

Pumice is a rock foam. When hot lava flows from a volcano, great patches of foam may form on the top or at the edges of the flow. This foam is really lava whipped up with bubbles of gas. After a while the foam hardens and the gas escapes, leaving air pockets all through the rock. Pumice looks like a sponge with very fine holes, but it is a rock nevertheless. If you toss a piece in water, it will float. The air pockets make pumice the lightest stone in the world.

The chances are you have met pumice at the dentist's without knowing it, for dentists use a pumice powder to clean teeth. Perhaps also you have met pumice in your kitchen—a good deal is ground up to go into scouring powders.

There is romance even in a can of scouring powder —if you know your rocks!

14

Patchwork Rocks

Dig down under the soil almost anywhere in the central part of our country and you will come first of all on patchwork rock. Indeed, under three-quarters of all the land in the world you would do the same.

To be sure, the rock isn't called patchwork rock. But that is what sedimentary rock mostly is. Most of it is made out of pieces worn away from older rocks. Sedimentary rock doesn't hold together because it was *cooked* together like the igneous rocks. It holds together because finer grains have filled in between its patches and pressure has *cemented* them together.

Let us take a close-up view of some of these rocks

made out of bits worn away from older rocks. And let us start with those that are made of the largest bits. *Conglomerate* is a rock that may have even big boulders in it. So let us begin with that.

The first glance tells us why this rock is called conglomerate. It is a conglomeration or mass of all sorts of things stuck together.

Our second glance shows us that all the rocks in the conglomerate are nicely rounded. We know what that means. It spells water. For only water could have worn stones down that way. They have either had a long, rough river journey or they have been battered and rolled by the waves of a lake or ocean.

But what *kind* of rock are they?

They may be any kind. Perhaps the larger pieces will be quartzite or granite. The smaller bits may be grains of quartz and feldspar. For all these materials are hard, and only durable stuff will take so much knocking about.

Our conglomerate may be made up of just little rocks or just big ones. Or it may be made up of fine materials with large stones stuck in it like plums in a Christmas pudding. If our conglomerate is like that, we will say, "This is *puddingstone.*"

But here is a rock that looks just like conglomerate except that the stones in it are sharp-edged. What kind of rock is this?

This is a *breccia*. The sharp edges tell us that these stones weren't carried far. They may have fallen into mud quite close to the spot where they broke off and been turned to rock right there.

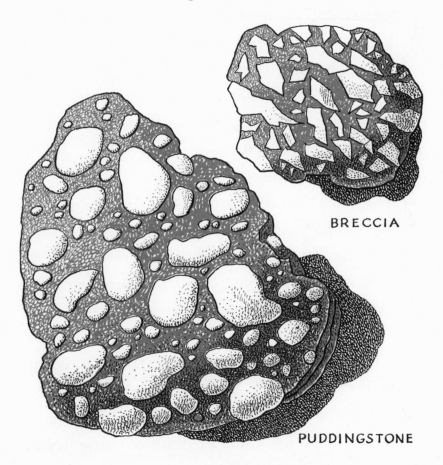

BRECCIA

PUDDINGSTONE

All About Our Changing Rocks

"Are they chips that weathered from a cliff and slid to the bottom?" we wonder. "Or were they dropped by a stream as it came sharply down into a valley? Or were these stones perhaps left behind by a melting glacier?"

But here, now, is a slab of sandstone. We don't have any trouble recognizing it. Just as its name tells us, we see that it is made of grains of sand and still finer particles that have been cemented together by pressure. We guess that the grains are quartz because sand is almost all quartz. But there may be some grains of feldspar, too, or some other minerals that can stand up under wear and tear.

Let us examine the cement (or finer particles) in our sandstone because cement is a very important part of the rock. It is largely the cement that gives color to sandstone—yellow, buff, brown, red, gray or green. How strong our rock is will also depend on the cement. If it is silica and there is plenty of it, our sandstone will be very strong. If the cement is something else and doesn't fill the pores completely, the rock will be weak.

Sandstone is a very useful rock. There are cities in which you will see block after block of houses with a sandstone front. Sometimes a whole town is all one color because so many of its buildings are made of one particular sandstone. The rock is easy to carve, too. So it is often made into trim for windows and doors.

Flagstone may be any rock that splits easily into large, flat slabs. But the flagstone we see is often sandstone. Once it paved many a sidewalk. Now we use concrete instead. But you can still see flagstone making stepping stones in lawns and gardens.

The purest sandstone is made into glass. In the Middle West there are great beds of such sandstone. It is used to make the very best glass. The St. Peter sandstone of Illinois and Missouri has been used in making many a bank window and many a pair of eyeglasses.

Now, sandstone may be coarse or it may be fine. As long as you can pick out the individual grains without a magnifying glass, the rock is still sandstone. After that it grades off into *siltstone*. And siltstone grades off into *shale*.

Here is a piece of shale. It is gray, the usual color. But shale may be many shades of pink and red. It can also be black, brown, buff and green. It may be made of clay or mud or both.

All About Our Changing Rocks

Our piece of shale is so soft we can cut it with a knife. When dry, it will crumble. Such soft shales are good only for making brick, tiles and cement. But there are hard shales, too. Here is one that has curious little pits all over its top, and here's another slab that has a wavy pattern over it.

Be careful! Treat these samples with care! They are museum pieces. The pits are the marks of rain-drops that fell millions of years ago. The wavy lines are ripple marks left by the waves of some vanished sea.

Waves of some ancient sea left ripple marks on many rocks.

15

What the Sea Left Behind

You may have heard that certain people have the mysterious power of finding water underground. They do it by means of a forked stick which they call a divining rod. The water diviner holds the two ends of the stick in his hands and walks along. Suddenly the stick starts twisting and turning in his hands. Then he announces that there is water under that spot.

People dig. Water comes up. Everybody thinks a miracle has been performed. But has it? Actually the people have been taken in by this so-called miracle. The water didn't come up because the diviner had a mysterious power. It came up because there is water under the ground almost everywhere—*if you dig and drill deep enough*. Some distance beneath the surface, the ground is saturated with water. There are even streams under the ground.

Some people claim to be able to find water with a divining rod.

All this hidden water is very hard working. And in one way it actually accomplishes more than surface water does; for underground water dissolves much vaster quantities of minerals out of the rocks. It can do that because it takes its time—instead of just *flowing over* the rocks, it *percolates* slowly *through* them.

Like surface water, underground water carries the dissolved minerals toward the sea. And there a most amazing thing happens. In the sea the dissolved minerals are turned into rock! This rock is sedimentary rock—but it is not like conglomerate, sandstone and shale. It is not made out of pieces worn away from older rocks. *It is made of materials that were once dissolved.*

"But how can that be?" you may ask. "If minerals are dissolved, how can they become solid again?"

If something happens to the water, they can become solid again. That is something you can prove to yourself by making a simple experiment.

Put salt in a glass of water and stir it. You will find that all the salt will dissolve—provided you haven't put in too much. The water will stay clear, it will remain the same color, but it will taste salty. So although you can't see it, you can be sure the salt is still there.

Now, what do you do to get it back into a solid?

You let the water evaporate.

When the water goes away, a ring of salt will appear on the glass.

That's one way of getting a dissolved mineral back into a solid—or making it *precipitate,* as a chemist would say. This way will always work with salt. But not with all minerals. Sometimes to get a precipitate you have to add something to the water. Just the presence of plants or animals—living or dead—in the water will make the minerals precipitate. And sometimes to get a precipitate you have to take something out of the water—carbon dioxide, for instance.

Now, perhaps you might think it would be a good idea to take sea water, evaporate it, and make salt that way. It would—if we didn't have such vast deposits of *rock salt*.

You have heard about *salt licks,* spots to which animals come to lick salt. These are places where salt deposits crop out on the surface. Much more of the rock salt lies under the ground. You would never guess from the size of the licks how much more of the rock lies under the surface.

There are beds of rock salt 400 feet thick in Kansas, Oklahoma, and Texas. Near Detroit the salt mines are more than 600 feet thick. In New York there are salt mines where the salt lies 300 feet thick and stretches for many miles. Tunnels are cut in solid salt, and rails are laid just as in any other mine. There will never be a shortage of salt in America, that's sure. We will never have to make salt out of sea water.

How did the salt get piled up like that?

Remember those seas that once rolled over America?

In a salt mine, rails are laid as in any other mine.

Well, they are responsible for our salt deposits.

Those seas went through many adventures. They came and went, came and went. But sometimes when the land was lifted up and the seas had to retreat to the ocean basins, an arm of the sea would get cut off and stay behind. That happened many times. Once it happened in the area that is now Michigan, New York and Pennsylvania. That was about a hundred million years before the Appalachians went up. It was hot and dry in the eastern part of our country then. The cut-off arm became a "dead sea." Slowly its water evaporated. And the salt was left.

Gypsum is another rock that was left behind when arms of the sea were cut off. There are vast deposits of gypsum in our country, and many of our states have gypsum mines. Oklahoma has so much of the rock that it is sometimes called the "gypsum state."

Gypsum is a fine-grained rock, generally white. But often it has impurities which color it gray, yellow, or even brick red. You will recognize it partly by the fact that it is so soft you can scratch it with your fingernail. It has only hardness 2.

You have almost certainly seen gypsum, though probably without knowing that it was gypsum. For a great deal of school chalk is made out of it. You also saw gypsum as plaster of Paris, in the form of a toy animal perhaps. Most gypsum goes into this plaster. To make it, the gypsum is first ground, then burned. The heat drives the water out of the rock. Then when you want to use the plaster, you put the water back in, mix, and pour the plaster into a mold. After a while the gypsum "sets." It is called plaster of Paris because from very early times it was made near Paris, France.

16

More
Rocks
From the Sea

There is another precipitated rock which you may have seen, probably without realizing that you were seeing it. When you were putting lime on your lawn to make the grass grow, you may have been spreading crushed *limestone*. You have also seen limestone in the form of concrete. You have seen rock wool, too, which is sometimes made of limestone. Perhaps the house you live in is insulated with it.

Limestone is so fine that your eyes won't be able to pick out the individual grains in the rock without a powerful magnifying glass. Yet this is one of the easiest rocks to recognize because it bubbles when vinegar is poured on it. Impurities often color the rock buff, brown, red, gray or green. But when it is pure, limestone is white or creamy. Many a fine public building has a floor or walls of limestone. Some of the Egyptian kings thought limestone so beautiful that they covered the pyramids with it. The royal tombs shone like huge gems in the dazzling desert sun.

Some of the pyramids are covered with slabs of limestone.

Always and forever limestone will make us think of Prehistoric Man. For the entrances to limestone caves were man's first permanent home.

It is very thrilling to go down under the earth into such a cave. Suddenly you find yourself in another

Limestone columns are still being formed in our caverns.

world. You are in a magic palace with walls of shining white. Room after room opens up before you. Some of the chambers are as huge as cathedrals. You look around, and everywhere you see great icicles of rock. They hang down from the ceiling. They rise from the floor. They are reflected from a pool of water at your feet. The pool is so motionless you think it is glass.

How were such huge, mysterious caverns as Mammoth Cave in Kentucky and the Luray Caverns in Virginia made?

Underground water made them. First a stream dissolved the limestone and hollowed out the chambers. Then the underground water changed its course and most of it went off to flow somewhere else. But that was only the beginning.

Drops of water kept percolating through cracks in the limestone above. Each drop was filled with calcite which it had dissolved out of the limestone over which it had traveled. So as the drop hung for a moment from the roof before it fell to the floor, it left a tiny bit of the calcite behind. Drop followed drop, bit was added to bit. And a rock icicle—a stalactite—grew downward from the ceiling.

From the place on the floor where the drops fell, an

upside down icicle—a stalagmite—grew up. Often the two finally met and formed a column. The icicles are still growing, the columns are still forming. They are walling off some of the chambers.

Was it such caverns that long ago made people think the earth was hollow inside? Perhaps. . . .

Limestone isn't all alike. As you know, some creatures have the power of taking lime out of water and turning it into shell. When the creatures die, their shells pile up on the sea bottom. Broken and ground-up bits of shell fill the spaces in between shells. Pressure cements everything together. And there you have *shell limestone* or *coquina.*

Whole shells can be seen in shell limestone or coquina.

All About Our Changing Rocks

One kind of shell limestone is made mostly of small, whole shells. Another is made mostly out of the remains of a fossil relative of the starfish. Another is made out of bits of coral. Still another has so much of a mineral called *dolomite* in it that it goes by that name. But none of these rocks is as familiar to us as *chalk*.

Chalk looks like a very fine white powder that has been pressed together. But real chalk is made almost entirely of the shells of animals so small that you can't see them except under a strong magnifying glass. If school chalk were real chalk, there would be countless millions of skeletons in a single stick such as we write with on the blackboard.

Once the animals that filled those tiny shells lived on the surface of the sea. Their dead bodies kept drifting down and settling on the bottom. For millions of years they did this. They fell and fell like an everlasting white rain. Now they are a rock thousands of feet thick. Pressure has cemented the tiny skeletons together. And the sea bottom has moved up.

Chalk is very soft. So it doesn't take long for water to wear it away. Twenty-five thousand years ago there was no English Channel. The place where it runs today was one vast bed of solid chalk that joined England and France. Stone Age Man could *walk* from one land to the other. In that little while water has eaten its way through the chalk and turned England and Scotland into an island. The White Cliffs of Dover are some of the last bits left, and the Channel is finishing them off fast. The tireless waves are battering the cliffs and wearing them away many feet every year.

Like limestone, chalk will always make us think of Prehistoric Man. For the very first mines in the world were made in chalk. Men of the Stone Age were looking for *flint*. They searched for it the way we search for metals.

Stone Age Man used flint for arrowheads and spear points.

All About Our Changing Rocks

It is easy enough to see why they wanted flint. Flint is a very hard rock—hardness 7. Yet it chips nicely and makes a very sharp cutting edge. Also it comes in a convenient size, for it is found most often as small chunks in chalk. For several hundred thousand years Prehistoric Man made most of his tools and weapons out of flint. A hundred thousand years ago he learned to strike fire with it.

Flint is similar to quartz. It is made out of silica that was once dissolved. The stone has a very fine grain and a waxy look and may be brown, or gray, or black. In our country it is not a common rock. Here *chert* took the place of flint. Chert is much like flint. Sometimes it comes in chunks—in limestone—and for this reason suited the Indians very well. It was just of a nice size to make into arrowheads.

17

Rocks
That Have
Changed

No one has ever found a piece of the earth's first crust. Of course, we can't help thinking that it must have been made of some kind of igneous rock. Reason tells us that you can't have rocks made out of patches until you have something to make patches out of.

But we can't prove it by the rocks because the very oldest ones we know show that they started out as sedimentary rocks. What kind we don't exactly know. For those old rocks have gone through so much since they were made that they are vastly changed. They have changed their shape, their hardness, and the size of their crystals. Some have lost minerals and had others

You can recognize gneiss by its streaky or banded look.

put in their place. Some have shifted their minerals around.

We call all rocks that have changed in any way *metamorphic*. This is the third great class of rocks. Every rock you find will be either igneous, sedimentary or metamorphic.

Now, it is not only sedimentary rocks that can change. *Any* rock can change. It can change a little or it can change a lot. It can go up a whole ladder of changes, or it can stop on any rung and stay there. It can also come back down the ladder. With more changes a rock can become simpler again.

Shale, for instance, can turn into *argillite*, which is a rock only a little harder and more compact than shale. But if the shale gets to the next rung of hardness, it will become *slate*. One rung more and it will be a *phyllite*. And finally it will be a *schist*.

But here is the strangest part of all. Different rocks can go through different changes, but *if they change enough, they finally end up looking very much alike.* Sandstone and granite are very different to start with. But they can both end up as schist.

You will remember Hutton's red granite that welled up into the cracks of the rock above. The magma had come up so hot that it had *baked* the rock on either side of the granite veins.

That is a way in which metamorphism, or change, very often happens. Rocks are baked when hot magma

From a lump of clay we mold a pot and bake it into pottery.

gets close to them. Which isn't surprising, for magma is much hotter than the inside of a roaring furnace. And we know what a roaring furnace will do to minerals. If we mold a pot out of clay—which was once feldspar—and put it in a kiln, the clay will bake into firm, hard, glassy pottery.

But baking is only a small part of the metamorphism of rocks. Hot water and steam do much more to change rocks. And so do pressure and movement.

When you rub your cold hands together, they get warm. That's primarily because friction makes heat. The same thing happens when you rub two rocks together—heat is created. So where rocks were folded, where they broke and slid and ground past each other, the greatest changes took place. The different minerals in the rocks sorted themselves out. New minerals also had to form that could adjust to the movement, the

In this metamorphic rock the minerals lie in sheets.

pressure and the heat. And the terrible pressure *made the minerals all lie in one direction*—in sheets or *folia*.

This made the rock over into something altogether different. For now it could split into thin leaves or slabs.

Let us take a look at gneiss, which is a rock that has been partly changed in this way. Gneiss looks much like granite as a rule. As a matter of fact, many gneisses started out as granite and are called *granite gneiss*.

In metamorphic rock different minerals sort themselves out.

There is generally a streaky or banded look about gneiss by which you can recognize it. The streaks, or bands, are there on account of the way the minerals have sorted themselves out. The light specks have all got together, and the dark specks have done the same. So first comes a light band of quartz and feldspar, then a thin, dark band of mica. Light and dark, light and dark—gneiss is like that. Sometimes the bands are straight, but more often they are crooked.

How easily the rock splits depends mostly on how much mica there is—the more the easier. That's because mica is flat and splits in sheets. But on the whole you will find that gneiss doesn't split easily.

With schists you will have no difficulty—all schists split easily.

Many schists started out as sedimentary rocks. But they have changed their name. The schist takes its name from the mineral that makes the folia or is the principal mineral. There is *quartz schist, talc schist, hornblende schist, mica schist,* and so on.

Mica schist is the commonest and is quite easy to recognize. When you break a piece, you will see flecks of mica sparkling in it. The mica and the quartz will run through the rock in thin, wavy layers. Very often garnets can be found in mica schist. Generally the garnet crystals have twelve faces, and their color may be red, yellow, brown, green or black. A deep red is very common.

Is metamorphism a bad or a good thing so far as man is concerned?

Garnets are often found in mica schist.

It is both. It can make a good, useful rock into one that is less useful. And it can also make a rock that isn't much use into one that is very useful.

For instance, there is sandstone, one of the best building stones we have. Sometimes sandstone gets squeezed so hard that it recrystallizes and turns into quartzite. It becomes a rock much harder than sandstone. And yet this quartzite isn't a good stone for building. It has been through so much squeezing that it is full of cracks.

With shale it's just the other way. Shale is usually soft and crumbly and not much use. But when it is metamorphosed into slate, it becomes extremely useful.

This stone house has a slate roof and a flagstone walk.

For slate is harder. And it will split into very thin slabs that are almost as smooth as the faces of crystals. This makes it excellent for roofing. It is good, too, for blackboards, switchboards, laboratory tables, and other surfaces where large, smooth, thin slabs are needed. Curiously, slate splits not *along* the layers but *across* them. This is so true of slate that we say of any rock that splits the same way, "It has slaty cleavage."

Limestone is another rock that has profited by change—it may be turned into *marble*. And marble is one of the most valuable rocks in the world.

The tests for this rock are just like the tests for limestone. It will fizz when you pour vinegar on it, and it can be easily scratched with a knife. Coarse kinds will look like lump sugar when you break the rock open.

Marble started out as shell limestone. It is the different colored shells and impurities that give the rock its different colors. Marble can be one color all over—white, gray, black, buff, yellow or red. Or it can be *marbled*—that is, the color can appear as irregular streaks or splotches. All kinds are wanted, all kinds are quarried. But it is the pure white marble that is most prized.

In part this is because pure marble can be quarried in thick blocks and won't split when it is carved. But in part it is because white marble is so beautiful and will take a high polish. There is really nothing more dazzling. The circular staircase of white marble in the Supreme Court Building in Washington is the show piece of the place. It is roped off and no one walks on it. It is there just for beauty, just to look at.

If granite is the King of Rocks, then marble is the Queen.

18

Museum in the Rocks

Around the year 1870, the newspapers got all excited about fossils. A Yale professor by the name of Othniel Marsh had taken a group of students out West to search the rocks for bones of animals that had lived millions of years ago. Buffalo Bill had gone along, too, to act as guide. And now the fossil hunters were shipping back carloads of rock full of stone bones. The scientists at Yale were busy chipping the bones out and putting them together. Every little while the papers had a picture of some fantastic creature the museum people had reconstructed.

"Can those fellows at Yale really know what they

are doing?" editors asked. "The rocks Marsh has sent back are a jumble of bones. They are like huge jig-saw puzzles. Maybe the pieces have been put together wrong. It certainly doesn't seem possible that such creatures ever lived in America."

But the scientists merely chuckled. They kept on reconstructing. They had never had such an exciting time before.

The picture of a dragon appeared in the papers. It was a flying reptile with a wing span of twenty feet. Then came birds with teeth. One which the museum people reconstructed was nearly as big as a man and had ninety-four sharp teeth in its mouth. Then came a dinosaur. Under the picture it said: "The Great and Terrible Lizard—Brontosaurus. Sixteen feet high, sixty-seven feet long."

Readers gasped. And they doubted. But finally they had to believe. Once creatures like that really had lived in America.

"What we can't understand, though," people said, "is how their bones got in the rocks!"

This was a question that had puzzled the world since the first fossil was found. How could living things, or traces of living things, get in the rock? How was it possible for the imprint of a leaf, or the footstep of a bird or beast, or the bones of a fish to get shut up like that?

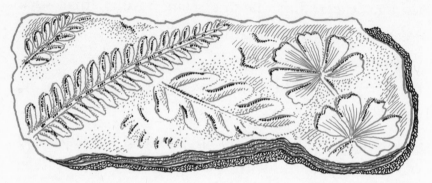

Occasionally leaves have left their imprint in rock.

For a long time men had tried to get around the mystery by saying that the bones and shells and other fossils they found in the rocks had never been living things at all.

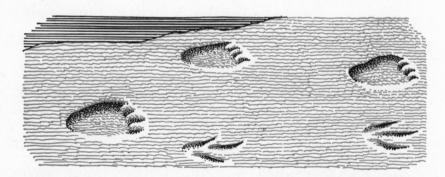

Footprints of ancient creatures are found in rock as well.

"Nature just made them for a joke," some people said.

"Or to decorate the rocks," said others.

Scholars argued: "There is a rock-making force in the earth that makes rock into forms resembling shells and bones."

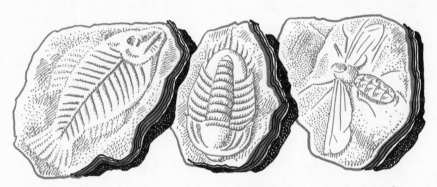

Through the years bones and shells were turned to rock.

Some argued that the fossils had indeed been living things once. "They *grew* inside the rocks," learned men explained, "from seeds that blew into the pores."

By the 1870s scientists had the true answer. By then they understood how rocks are made so there was no longer any mystery about how the fossils had got in.

"They got in *before* the rocks were finished," the scientists explained. "The bones and things got in when the rocks were still in the making, when they were just loose sediments. Those sediments were then the surface on which plants and animals lived or on which they fell or were dropped when they died. Sand and mud filled in and covered over the tracks which creatures made as they walked and crept and burrowed. Sand and mud covered up the bones and shells and leaves. It was long afterward that the sediments turned to rock."

"But so many plants and animals have lived and died," people argued. "Why aren't all the rocks full of fossils? Why don't any of us find them when we split a rock open?"

"Well, in the first place," the scientists answered, "by no means *all* the plants and animals that lived and died got into the rocks. Only one in many millions did. Sometimes not even that many. Because, you see, it takes very special conditions to make a fossil. A living thing that has no hard parts has only a ghost of a chance to become a fossil. It just decays and there's nothing left. And even creatures with hard parts like shells and bones don't have a chance to become fossils unless they are buried quickly.

"Just think of all the millions of buffalo that once lived and died and left their bodies on our plains.

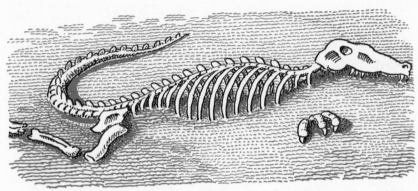

A skeleton, not covered by sand or mud, is unlikely to become a fossil.

Except for a bone or a horn here and there, nothing is left. For no sooner did a creature die than wolves and vultures ate it. Sun and rain and bacteria destroyed what was left. Roots got in the cracks of the bones and helped to break them up. They turned to dust.

"No, if you want to find fossils, look in places where water has been. When creatures are drowned, their bodies sink to the bottom where they are soon covered by sand and mud. That preserves them from enemies. Look for fossils in rocks that were once the bottom of a river or a lake or a shallow sea. Look for fossils in sedimentary rock that was laid down by water."

And then the scientists would talk about the wonderful natural history museum in the rocks. The shells and bones in the museum were pretty well scrambled, they admitted. They weren't in order by any means. But at least the rocks had kept the *Record of Living Things.*

"And if it weren't for that record," the scientists said, "we would know scarcely anything about the plants and animals that lived before human beings were here to see them.

"Of course," they added, "the rocks didn't keep a sample of *everything* that ever lived. Or, at least, we haven't found it yet. But they kept a lot. They kept enough so we can piece out a very good picture of what happened—in spite of the gaps. Some pages of the record are missing and some pages are blurred, but the story for the most part is clear. And *we* think there is none more strange or wonderful."

19

Reading the Record

How does the *Record of Living Things* read?

Life is very, very old, the record says, but it is not so old as the rocks. Our oldest rocks were perhaps a thousand million years old before the first living things appeared.

They were insignificant living things when they did appear. They had no hard parts. They left almost nothing of themselves behind. We find traces of carbon that may mean simple plants were living a thousand million years ago. We find fossil burrows which tell us that here a worm crawled under the mud. That's nearly all. The first chapter isn't very exciting.

Strange creatures lived in the sea millions of years ago.

The second starts off better. All of a sudden a whole lot of different forms are on the scene.

We read, and a picture of the shallow sea springs up before us. Seaweeds, moored in the mud, wave gently to and fro. Worms crawl and burrow. Sponges, each like a delicate vase, capture and swallow tiny prey. Shell armor has just been developed, and the sea floor is thick with shelled creatures.

There are flat shells and round shells, fan-shaped and coiled, smooth shells and fluted and knobby shells. And groveling on the sea floor among them are flat,

odd-shaped creatures that look like great wood lice
but wear a lobster-like crust on their backs. These are
the trilobites, the biggest animals the world had known
at that time. They are less than four inches long, most
of them, but still in this world of lowly creatures they
are Kings of the Sea.

What of the land? Is there nothing of land life in
the record the rocks have kept?

Not yet. That is to come. For the time being, the
sea triumphs over the land. Water covers the continents. The rocks still speak of the sea.

The rocks tell us that the first fish had an armor of shell.

But the sea is different now. It is teeming with star-
tling new creatures. There are animals now built on
an entirely different plan. They have something no
creature in the world has had before—a bony frame
*in*side the body. The muscles are attached to the skeleton and can move it around. It is a wonderful plan
for speed.

The new animals are bigger, too. No longer are
trilobites Kings of the Sea. There are sharks twenty
feet long. They get around fast. But some of the fishes
don't put their trust in speed. They haven't laid aside
the old armor of shell. Some are so weighted down by
it that they can't get around. They lie on the sea bottom with their four-foot mouths wide open, waiting
for prey to come close. Then *snap!* go the terrible
jaws. They can bite a shark in half.

But now the land is rising, mountains are being
formed. Living things are flourishing on the land at
last.

There are lush forests, though not of such trees as
we know today. The great-great-grandparents of our
pines are here, towering 120 feet above the swamp.
The ancestors of our palms are here. They are nearly
as tall and boast a hundred different kinds. There are

Some day these trees and ferns and rushes will die. Eventually they will be turned into the rock that we call coal.

fountain-like seed ferns carrying little nuts under the leaves. There are tree ferns with fronds five and six feet long. There are scouring rushes that look exactly like our horsetails but stand thirty feet high.

Some day these trees and ferns and rushes will die and turn to muck. The muck will turn to peat. The peat will turn to rock. And two-legged creatures as yet undreamed of will call the rock *coal*.

The air is warm and humid—things shoot up overnight. Everything is big, even the insects. Cockroaches four inches long crawl among the damp roots. Dragonflies with a wingspread of nearly thirty inches dart in the open parts of the forest.

The zoom of their wings is not the only sound in the swamp. There are sprawling four-footed creatures here trying out the land. They haven't taken to it fully yet. But they do walk after a fashion. They do breathe air. And they have a voice. It is the first voice in the world.

Some day it will burst into the song of birds. But there are no birds yet. There will be none for many millions of years yet. Before the birds come, the swamp forests will go. There will be change and change and change.

20

Blurred
and
Missing Pages

What is the meaning of so much change? Why did so many kinds of living things pass out, never to come back again?

The rocks tell us sometimes. But sometimes they have no answer for us. We rack our brains to find an explanation and end up asking, "Why?"

It is that way with the dinosaurs. "Why did they die out?" we ask. "Why isn't there a single dinosaur in the world today?"

It seems unbelievable as we read the record of the rocks. We see the dinosaurs come on shortly after the warm age of the swamp forests is over. They are little fellows at first, most of them no bigger than a cat or a crow, the biggest not more than twelve feet long. We see them making themselves at home in the uplands

The first dinosaurs were no bigger than a cat or a crow.

of New England and New Jersey. We don't suspect that these reptiles, running like birds on two feet, and their brothers, walking around on four, are going to take the world over. But suddenly we see a strange thing happen. We see the dinosaurs begin to grow.

They grow and they grow and they grow. They get to be tremendous. They get to be the biggest creatures on earth. Some of the two-legged ones are forty-seven feet long and stand twenty feet high. Their brothers of the swamp are sixty-seven feet long and more. They are so heavy that the earth trembles when they pass.

Some of the reptiles go in for bony armor plate. Some go in for horns and claws. Some go in for terrible teeth. But all are monstrous. The world is a nightmare of unbelievable monsters. They take over the land, they take over the sea, they take over the air. Dragons with a wingspread of twenty-four feet darken the sky. Monsters fifty feet long rule the seas. On the

Reptiles took over the land, the sea and the sky.

land there is everlasting war. Teeth and claws and horns tear and rip and thrust, feet trample, tails lash.

Then suddenly the record of the dinosaurs ends. There isn't a dinosaur left. It's just as though a curtain went down.

We search the rock record. "What happened?" we ask. "Did the climate change? Did the plant-eating monsters have nothing left to feed on? Did the flesh eaters eat up the others and then one another? Did enemies with better brains appear?"

We know that creatures which can't adapt themselves to new conditions die out. But what conditions couldn't the dinosaurs adapt themselves to? What killed them off?

The rocks don't say. All they do is show us a newly created world. The scenery is different. The animals are different.

And there's the most confusing part of it—the new animals are such as couldn't possibly be a threat to the monsters. Besides, the new creatures aren't really new. They've been around for some time only we didn't notice them, they were so small. They have been keeping out of the way of the stomping feet and lashing tails of the dinosaurs.

The modern world was just right for mammals.

Now that their enemies are gone, the little mammals came down from the trees. They crawl out of their holes. They take over the earth. For the modern world that unfolds is exactly to their liking.

There is plenty of food for all, plenty of shelter. New things are growing all over the world. Wonderful seed-bearing grasses cover the ground. Wonderful fruit and nut-bearing trees with net-veined leaves rustle among the evergreens. There are beeches and birches, maples and oaks, sweet gums and tulip trees. Laurel, ivy, hazelnut and holly flourish. A thousand flowers bloom. A thousand insects fly and crawl and hop. Birds sing.

We look at the little animals as they step out into the

Flowers and grasses may record their story in the rocks.

modern world and we think: "Is it possible? Are these the creatures that will develop into horses and elephants and rhinoceroses, cattle and deer, dogs, cats, monkeys, and men?"

They are so puny! They are so slow! They all have short legs and flat feet and long jaws! And they are all so dull! A hedgehog has as much sense. Is it possible that these creatures will inherit the earth?

We search the rocks. "The little mammals went through many stages," they tell us. "See, we've caught samples of some of the creatures as they developed. Here is a horse only eleven inches high. Here is an elephant not waist-high to a man. Here is a camel no bigger than a jack rabbit."

Seventy-five million years is long. There is plenty of time for the little mammals to get bigger. There is plenty of time for them to get smarter. There is time for the horse to get up on one toe; for the elephant to get a trunk; for the camel to grow his hump; for the whale to take to the sea and the bat to conquer the air. Even a million years is long. It took only a million years for man to develop.

"And is man the end of the record?" you ask.

There is no end. As long as there are living things on earth the rocks will keep on recording them. No one can even guess what forms will yet appear. But this we know—some of them, at least, will get into the rocks.

Some Common
Rock-Forming Minerals

Calcite

Calcite is the most abundant mineral in the world after quartz. Limestone and marble are largely calcite. It has a bright or glassy appearance. Usually it is colorless, but impurities may color it pink, yellow, brown, green, or blue. The streak of calcite is colorless. Hardness is 3. It bubbles when vinegar is poured on it.

Calcite has more than 2,500 different crystal shapes, but the crystals always group themselves in sets of three. The crystals split easily in three directions, never at right angles. However, most calcite forms no crystals at all.

Iceland spar is pure, transparent calcite. It has what is called double refraction. That is, it bends light in such a way that you see double when you look through it. This alone is enough to identify it.

Some varieties of calcite take their name from the shape of their crystals. There is *dogtooth spar* and *nailhead spar*. *Satin spar* is called that because it consists of satiny-looking fibers.

Dolomite

Dolomite is like calcite in appearance. It is usually white or gray, but occasionally it is flesh-colored. Its streak is colorless. Dolomite is a little harder than calcite—almost hardness 4.

Feldspar

Feldspar, which means field stone, names a group of minerals that are much alike. There is more quartz

Calcite (Dogtooth Spar)   Dolomite

in the world than there is any one feldspar. But the feldspars as a group are five times as common as quartz. Feldspar is always a part of granite and other igneous rocks. The most common colors are white or gray, pale pink or pale yellow, but feldspar may also be olive-green or brown. Streak is white or colorless. Hardness is 6. Feldspar gleams more like china than glass. All feldspars will split clean into blocks with smooth sides that lean a little to one side.

All feldspars are made of aluminum, silicon and oxygen. But each has one or more other elements. Orthoclase, microcline, and plagioclase are names of some common feldspars. They are not easy to tell apart and it is enough to identify them as feldspar.

Gypsum

Gypsum is colorless, white, or pale yellow, gray or pink. Streak is white. Hardness is 2. Gypsum is in layers between various kinds of sedimentary rocks. But it more commonly forms thick beds of rock between salt beds. When gypsum is heated, the water evaporates. If water is added, gypsum recrystallizes.

Halite

Halite, or table salt, is colorless, white, or reddish

and may be transparent to semi-transparent. Halite has a salty taste, which is the surest test for it. Hardness is between 2 and 3. It will cleave perfectly into cubes, being made up of crystals of that shape.

Hornblende

Hornblende belongs to the minerals called amphiboles found in granitic and metamorphic rocks. Hornblende has a pearly or silky look and the color is usually black. Streak is colorless or a very pale tint. Hardness is 5 to 6. The crystals are six-sided. Hornblende looks so much like pyroxene that it is hard to tell them apart. But hornblende splits more easily. When found in schist, it often has needle-like crystals that give the rock a fibrous look. Pyroxene never has this form.

Feldspar   Gypsum Halite   Hornblende

All About Our Changing Rocks

Mica

Mica is the name of a common group of minerals that can be split into sheets as thin as paper. The size of the sheet that can be peeled off depends on the size of the crystal. You can bend a sheet of mica, but as it is elastic, it will spring right back. Hardness is 2 to 3. Usually mica has a pearly look, but the color varies. Streak is white.

Muscovite, or white mica, is generally colorless but may be light gray or green or brown. It is transparent. Muscovite occurs in granite along with quartz and feldspar and in gneiss and mica schist. Movie snowstorms and Christmas-tree snow are muscovite.

Biotite, or black mica, is generally dark green, brown or black. It is common in granites and many gneisses and schists. Biotite is just a little harder than muscovite. In granite you can tell it from hornblende because you can scrape biotite off with your fingernail.

Olivine

Olivine is a mineral found in dark igneous rocks such as basalt. It is olive-green in color. Hardness is between 6 and 7. It looks glassy. When it cleaves, it leaves the surface looking like shells.

Some Common Rock-Forming Minerals

Pyroxene

Pyroxene is a group of minerals much like the amphiboles. Both are composed of the same substances, have the same hardness (5 to 6), the same colors (usually black, green, or gray), and the same pearly or silky look. But pyroxene makes a white or gray-green streak. It doesn't always split easily. And its crystals are eight-sided and shorter and stouter than those of the amphiboles.

Quartz

Quartz, the world's most common *single* mineral, has many varieties. Most sands and sandstones are quartz and many veins are filled with milky quartz. In granite it looks like bits of glass. Quartz is colorless or white, but impurities may make it yellow, red, pink,

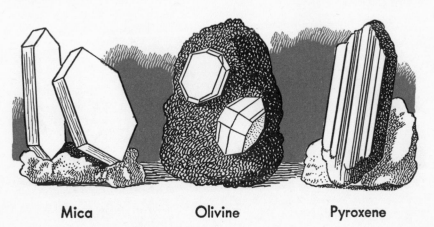

Mica   Olivine   Pyroxene

purple, green, blue, brown or black. Streak is white or very light colored. It runs from transparent to opaque. Hardness is 7. Most quartz does not form crystals and splits in such a way that it leaves the surface looking like shells.

Sulfur

Sulfur is always yellow. Much of it is in earthy masses but it also forms brittle, shining crystals which look like resin. Hardness is 2. It is very light weight, melts very easily, and burns with a blue flame and a suffocating smell. The mineral often comes up with magma and is deposited in the craters of volcanoes. Much was laid down in shallow seas, however. One huge deposit —100 to 125 feet thick—was laid down deep under what is now Louisiana and Texas.

Quartz   Sulfur

Talc

Talc is a very soft mineral—hardness 1. Yellow, gray, or apple green. Streak is white. Talc rarely forms crystals, but occurs in flaky masses. It has a greasy or soapy feel, and an impure form of talc is even called "soapstone."

Talc

Index

Index

Index